CARD GAMES &
TRICKS

BY
Patrick Page

MACDONALD

First published 1982

Macdonald and Co. Publishers
Holywell House
Worship Street
London EC2A 2EN

© Macdonald and Co 1982
ISBN 0 356 06344 5 (paperback)
ISBN 0 356 06384 4 (hardback)

Printed by New Interlitho
Milan, Italy

About this book

This book has been carefully planned to help you become an expert. Look for the special pages to find the information you need. **PROJECT** pages, with a **grey border**, suggest some interesting ideas for things to do and make. At the end of the book there is a useful **REFERENCE** section.

A note to readers: we all know that boys *and* girls play card games and perform tricks. To avoid writing 'he/she' all the way through the book we have just used 'he' or 'she'.

A popular pastime

Playing card games is probably one of the most popular pastimes in the world today. You'll find a deck of cards in most homes everywhere.

A simple game of cards combines two elements which have always fascinated people – chance and skill.

Introduced into Britain over 600 years ago

No one knows exactly who invented playing cards but it seems likely that they were first introduced into Britain in the 14th century. At this time they were more or less a copy of existing French cards.

The cards were all handpainted and the nobility were the only ones to use them. They were the only people wealthy enough to be able to afford them!

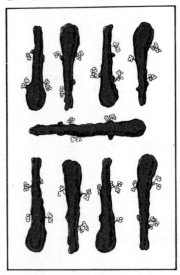

The Nine of Clubs (Bastos) from an old Spanish pack. The name stayed but the shape changed.

An artist's impression of the *Six of Birds* by the Master Engraver, Strasburg 1450.

In the first part of this book you'll find a selection of card games for small groups of people plus examples of games for one player.

The second half of this book is full of card tricks which will give you with an insight into the workings of the card manipulator.

The Joker is the modern version of the Fool in the old Tarot cards, which was the extra card in the deck.

Cheap and easy to carry

Card tricks have always fascinated magicians and audience alike. From the performer's point of view, cards are inexpensive, easy to carry and tricks can be performed almost at the drop of a hat!

From the audience's viewpoint, a few simple card tricks gives the performer an instant reputation for dexterity and amazing skill.

If you practise for a while you can have great fun plus an enlarged reputation because of your newly acquired skill!

Cards through the ages

Playing cards were engraved for the first time around 1445 and were probably produced near Basle, Switzerland. This is deduced from the styles of clothing on the picture cards. Here are a few samples of European playing cards still in use today.

German Cards

Poker-size Spanish Cards

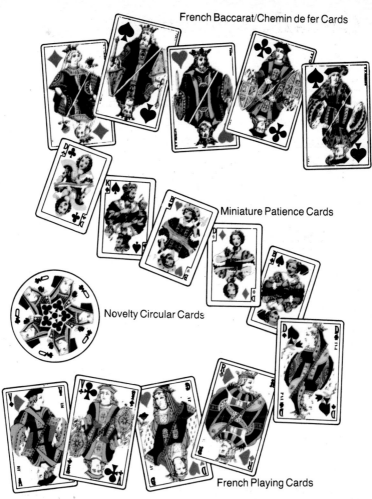

French Baccarat/Chemin de fer Cards

Miniature Patience Cards

Novelty Circular Cards

French Playing Cards

How did we get the four suits of Clubs, Hearts, Spades and Diamonds? They appear to be a mixture of cards from Italy, Spain, Germany and France.

The Spanish cards had Clubs (which were actual wooden clubs), Coins, Cups and Swords. The Italian cards were the same.

The French cards had Hearts, Pikes, Carreaux (which are paving tiles) and Trefoils (which are a sort of three leaf clover).

The German cards had Hearts, Acorns, Bells and Leaves.

The English took the French Trefoil but called it after the Spanish Club. They took the Pike, altered it a little and added the Spanish word for sword (Espada) and this became the Spade.

The Heart came from either the French or German. Diamonds may have been derived from the French paving tile or from the Italian and Spanish gold coins. (Denari in Italy, Oros in Spain, which then became Diamonds in Britain.)

7

Card techniques

If you are going to play cards or perform a few card tricks, it is essential that you should be able to handle a deck of cards properly. Study the illustrations which follow and you should be able to shuffle and cut cards in a short space of time.

The Riffle shuffle
Hold the deck in the right hand as shown. Allow half of the deck to release itself by springing the cards slightly, so that approximately half of the deck is resting on the tips of the left fingers.

Take this half of the deck in the left hand, so that you now have half the deck in exactly the same position in each hand and bend them as shown by applying pressure with the forefingers on to the back of each packet.

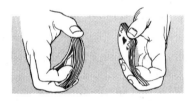

Now allow the cards to riffle downwards on to the table top, the cards from both packets being released at the same time. The cards will automatically interleave.

Once the cards are exhausted, push the interleaved cards together and square them up.

The Overhand shuffle
Hold the deck in the right hand between the thumb and four fingers.

The left thumb now approaches the deck and starts to pull the cards off the top of the deck in small packets which are gathered in the left hand until all the cards in the right hand are exhausted.

This should be repeated several times.

Cutting the deck
When playing cards, the deck should always be shuffled before each game starts. It is also customary to offer the deck to another player and ask him to 'cut the deck'.

The deck is placed on the table. A portion of the deck is lifted off the top of the deck and placed to one side. The remainder of the deck is now lifted from the table and placed on top of the first portion.

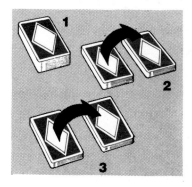

Dealing

First, the dealer shuffles the cards and offers the deck to the player on the right and asks him or her to cut the deck. The dealer then picks up the deck and starts to distribute the cards to the players.

Starting with the person on the left the dealer gives one card to each player until everyone (including the dealer) has a card. This is repeated until each player has the correct number of cards for the game.

If the game is one in which each player takes a turn dealing, it is usual for the deal to travel in a clockwise direction.

Card Games

Snap

The Players This is one of the easiest games of all to learn. Any amount of players may play, but the ideal number would be from two to four players.

The Deal The whole deck of cards is dealt out to the players who pick up their cards and hold them face down in their hands. Looking at the faces of the cards is not allowed.

The Play Starting with the dealer, each player deals one card face up in the centre of the table, making a pile of cards.

This is continued until one player deals one card on top of another player's card, which is of the same colour and value. e.g. two black sevens. When this happens the first player to call out "Snap" wins.

This player now adds the pile of cards in the centre of the table to the bottom of the packet of cards he already holds.

The first player to win all the cards in the deck in this way is the winner of the game.

The Memory Game

The Players Any number of players may play.
The Deal After the cards have been thoroughly
shuffled, they are spread around haphazardly on the
table top, face down.
The Play The first player on the dealer's left now
turns any two cards face up. If the player turns up two
cards of the same value, such as two sixes, he places
the cards face down in front of him. This player now
turns up another two cards. If these are a pair they are
placed in front of him.

If two cards are turned up which are not a pair, the
player turns them face down again where they are.
It is now the next player's turn.

Once all the cards have been paired, the player
with the most pairs is the winner.

As play progresses, the players will try to
remember where certain cards are on the table top
and try to pair them with other cards which have not
been exposed.

Put and Take

The Players From two to six players can play this game.

The Deal We will assume that there are six players. The dealer deals out five cards to each player but none to herself.

After the players have picked up their cards, the dealer now deals herself five cards, one at a time, face up in front of her.

The Play After the dealer has dealt herself the first card face up, any player who has a card of the same value 'puts' one sweet into the centre of the table. This is repeated with the remaining four cards.

After the dealer has dealt the five cards, they are gathered up and placed on the bottom of the deck. The dealer now deals herself another five cards one at a time as before, but this time, any player who has a similar card 'takes' one sweet from the centre of the table.

Any sweets left on the table are taken by the dealer. If there are no sweets left on the table when a player has to 'take' one, the dealer must supply them from her own private stock.

The deal is now passed to the next player.

Pairs

The Players This is a game for one player.

The Deal Nine cards are dealt out on the table in three rows of three. If any of these cards form a pair they are picked up and placed aside out of play.

The Play Any places left vacant by the removal of a pair are filled by dealing that number of cards from the remainder of the deck. If any of these cards help to form a pair, the pair is removed from play as before.

If there are no pairs or spaces available the remaining cards of the deck are dealt on to the nine cards one at a time, starting at the top left hand corner and dealing across from left to right. This is repeated with the remaining two rows.

As soon as any card you have dealt forms a pair with any other card, the pair is removed from play.

You cannot at any time form a pair with another card which is below the card you have dealt. It can only be paired with a card from another pile.

The Object The object of the game is to pair off the entire deck. You will often reach a stage where it is impossible to pair off any cards. When this happens, the deck is reshuffled and you start again.

Donkey

The Players Any number of players from three to thirteen may play.

The Pack If there are five players you only use the Aces, Kings, Queens, Jacks and Tens. If there are seven players you add the Nines and Eights so that there are only four cards for each player. Any remaining cards in the deck are placed aside and not used in the game.

Counters You will also require a number of counters, matchsticks or sweets. A number of sweets are placed in the centre of the table, one fewer than the number of players. So, if there are five players, four sweets are placed on the table.

The Play As soon as the dealer says 'go', each player starts passing cards one at a time to the player on his or her left.

The first player who manages to collect a complete set of four cards of the same number value picks up one of the sweets. The moment this happens, all the other players make a grab for the sweets and take one each. Because there is one sweet less than players, one player will not have a sweet. This player is Donkey.

The first player to collect a set of four cards of the same value must show the cards. If that player doesn't show the cards, he or she becomes the Donkey.

The Scoring A pencil and paper score is kept and each time a player becomes Donkey one letter of the name of the game is added to their score.

The first player to score D-O-N-K-E-Y is the Donkey. He or she must then stand up and call out Hee Haw three times!

Old Maid

The Players Three or more players may play.
The Pack One of the Queens is removed from the deck and placed aside face up so that only 51 cards remain.
The Deal The whole deck of cards is dealt out between the players. It is not important that the cards do not deal out evenly.
The Object The object of the game at this point is to discard all the cards in your hand which are pairs.
The Play If you have two nines in your hand you place them on the table in front of you, face down.

All the players discard their pairs immediately after the cards have been dealt. Three cards alike are not allowed, only pairs. As soon as all the players have discarded their pairs, the person on the dealer's left takes one card from the dealer's hand, without looking at the dealer's hand. This card is added to the existing hand and if it makes a matching pair, the player discards the pair face down on the table.

The next player to the left now removes a card from the previous player's hand and this is repeated continuously round the table. When a player draws a card which makes a pair, both cards are discarded.

This play is continued until only one player is left with one card, which will be an unmatched Queen. This Queen is the 'Old Maid'.

The Scoring A pencil and paper score is kept and after perhaps ten or fifteen games, the player with the fewest Old Maids is the winner.

Speedy Solitaire

The Players A game for one player.
(This is probably one of the easiest of all games of
solitaire.)
The Deal Shuffle the cards thoroughly and hold them
face down. Now deal the cards one at a time face up in
a pile on the table in front of you.

As you deal the cards count 'one, two, three, four,
five, six, seven, eight, nine, ten, jack, queen, king'.
This is repeated four times until you have run
through all 52 cards in the deck.

The Object The object is to go straight through the 52
cards without ever calling out the same card you are
dealing. If you call out 'four' and the card you are
dealing is a four, gather up all the cards and give the
deck a shuffle and start again.

Auld Lang Syne

The Players This is a game for one player.
The Play The four Aces are placed in a row along the top of the table.

Four cards are now dealt in a row in front of the four Aces. If there are any Two's among those four cards they are removed and placed on top of the Aces. Suits are not important.

Another four cards are dealt on top of the first four or in any spaces which have been created.

The idea is to build up sequences of cards on top of the Aces. Remember, suits are not important.

The cards are always dealt out four at a time and as they become available they are removed and placed on top of the Aces, until four packets of thirteen cards have been built up on the Aces.

If the whole deck has been dealt out and no further play is possible the game is abandoned. The cards are now gathered up and a new game is started.

Simple Rummy

Simple Rummy

The Players Two to four people is the ideal number of players for this game.

The Object Played with seven cards each, the object of the game is to divide the seven cards into two sets of three and four cards, e.g. three Queens and four Twos; three Tens and Four, Five, Six, Seven of the same suit or Seven, Eight, Nine, Ten of the same suit plus Jack, Queen, King of another suit.

The Deal The dealer (starting with himself) deals each player seven cards and on the last round deals himself one extra card, so that he has eight cards.

The remaining cards are placed in the centre of the table. When each player has seven cards they are held so that no one else can see them.

The Play The dealer with eight cards, discards one of them face up on the table. The next player can pick up this card and add it to her own set if it will improve the chances of making Rummy.

If the player decides to keep this card she must discard (face up) one of the cards she is holding.

If she decides that the dealer's discard is of no value she picks up one card from the central packet.

She can either keep this card and discard another or discard the new card immediately.

It is now the next player's turn. He also has a choice of picking up the discard or taking a card from the central packet. This is continued round and round the table, each player having the same choice.

The first player who achieves two sets (one of three cards and one of four cards) is the winner.

Alternative Hand

Another 'Hand' If you are playing
for matchsticks, sweets or even a
pencil and paper points system,
there is one other 'hand' which can
call Rummy.

This is where the player has
managed to accumulate seven
cards of the same suit in a row.
These could be the A, 2, 3, 4, 5, 6,

7 of Hearts or 5, 6, 7, 8, 9, 10, J of
Spades.

The Scoring In this case the
losing players have to pay the
winning player double the stake, or
in the case of a points system the
winning player is awarded double
the normal number of points.

Variation using an Ace

Variation Instead of just having to
accumulate one set of three cards
and one set of four cards, it is
possible to have two sets of three
cards only, plus one Ace.

War

The Players This is a very good game for two players only.

The Deal The deck is dealt out one card at a time to each player until they have twenty-six each. Each player places his packet of cards face down on the table in front of him, without looking at the faces.

The Play Each player turns the top card of his packet face up and places it on the table.

The player who has the highest value card in front of him picks up both face up cards and adds them to the bottom of his face down packet.

Aces are highest value, Two's are lowest value.

If two cards of the same value are turned up, they are left on the table. Both of the players now place another card on top of the first two cards but this time the cards are face down.

Another two cards are placed face up on top of the face down cards and the card of the highest value wins. The winner then picks up all the cards.

If these last two cards are of the same value, two more cards are placed on top of them face down and still another two cards face up. Again the card of the highest value wins.

This is continued until one player wins all the cards. If a player runs out of face down cards but still has some face up, he turns them face down and continues play.

Twenty-Nine

The Players A game suitable for four players.
The Deal All fifty-two cards are dealt out so that each player has thirteen cards.
The Play The player to the dealer's left starts play by placing one card face up on the table, and as he does so he calls out the name of the card e.g. 'seven'.

The next player plays a card which is for example, a nine. She adds the nine to the previous player's value and calls 'sixteen'.

If the next player plays a four, this is added to the previous total and the player calls 'twenty'.

This is repeated round and round the table until one player plays a card which makes the total twenty-nine. When this happens, this player scoops up all the face up cards.

No one is allowed to play a card which brings the total beyond twenty-nine. If a player cannot play a card which takes the total to twenty-nine or below, he passes.

All picture cards count as ten. If a player loses all his cards he drops out of the game. The winner is the player who captures all the cards.

Rolling Stone

The Players Five or six players are the ideal number for this game.

The Deal The whole deck is dealt out between the players. The fact that some players get one more card than others is not important.

The Play The player to the dealer's left starts off by playing one card face up. The remaining players now have to play a card of the same suit. If everyone plays a card of the same suit, these cards are gathered up and placed aside.

The player who played the highest card now plays another card. Again, everyone has to play a card of the same suit.

The first player who cannot play a card of the same suit, picks up all the cards that have been played and adds them to the cards he is holding. The same player now plays a card to which the others must follow suit.

Play continues in this fashion and the first player to dispose of all his cards is the winner.

Animals

The Players This is another game which is ideal for four players.

The Deal The whole deck is dealt out so that each player has thirteen cards. The players put their cards face down in front of them. No one is allowed to look at their cards.

The Play All four players now adopt the names of animals. No two players can have the same animal name.

The player to the dealer's left starts off play by turning the top card of her packet face up on the table alongside the packet. Each player now takes a turn at turning the top card of his packet face up.

If two cards of the same denomination turn up, the first player of the two to call out the animal name of the other player wins the other player's card.

If three or four cards of the same denomination show up the same rule applies – the names of the other two or three players have to be called out.

Cards are continuously dealt face up until two cards of the same denomination show up. Each time, the winner takes all the face up cards of the other player, and adds them to the bottom of his own packet.

If a player runs out of face down cards, he turns all his face up cards over and continues play. If a player loses all of his cards he drops out of play.

The player who gains all fifty-two cards is the winner.

Simple Fan Tan

The Players Three or more players can play this simple version of Fan Tan.

The Deal The full deck is dealt out between the players. It is not important that (because of the number of players) the cards are not dealt out equally.

The Play The player on the dealer's left starts play by playing any card. Assuming that it is the Four of Clubs, the idea is for the next player to play the Five of Clubs on top of the Four. If he doesn't have the Five, he passes. This is continued until someone plays the Five.

Players who pass place one sweet into a central pool. Each player now has the opportunity to play the Six of Clubs, then the Seven and so on.

When the King of Clubs is reached play continues with the Ace, Two etc. The player who plays the last card of a suit has the privilege of playing the first card of a new suit.

The player who disposes of all his or her cards first is the winner and collects the central pool of sweets plus one sweet for every card the other players are holding.

Variation Instead of the player on the dealer's left being the first to play by leading off with the card of his or her choice, sometimes the dealer will turn the very last card face up and whoever has the Ace of that suit begins the play.

If the card turned face up is an Ace then the player holding the Two of that suit leads off the play.

Players who pass are allowed to use the face up card if they need it.

Switch

The Players This is an ideal game for four players.

The Deal Each player is dealt five cards. The remainder of the deck is placed in the centre of the table face down.

    The top card of this packet is placed face up alongside it. This is the starter card. If it is an Ace, bury it in the centre of the packet and turn the next card face up.

The Object The object of the game is to lose your cards as quickly as possible. The first player to do so is the winner.

The Play The player to the dealer's left starts off by playing a card face up on top of the starter card. It must be a card of either the same value or suit as the starter card. Each player follows by playing a card which is either the same suit or value as the previous card.

If a player is unable to play a card because he has no cards of the same value or suit as the previous card, he must draw a fresh card from the packet on the table and add it to his hand. The player must continue to draw cards until one is found which can be played.

The game ends as soon as one player has lost all his or her cards.

If a block is reached when no one can play a card of the same suit or value, the game is abandoned and a new game started.

Using the Ace

A player who cannot play a card (of the same suit or value as the previous card) but has an Ace, can play the Ace instead and at the same time call SWITCH. He must also call the name of the suit he is switching to. The next player must remember and watch the suit.

Using the Ace means that a player can change the suit of the cards to be played to any other suit they wish. If the player wants to use his Ace it is a good idea to change to a suit that he holds most of.

Highland Fling

The Players This is a simple form of whist and any number of players from two to seven may play.

The Deal The dealer deals seven cards to each player and turns the next card face up in the centre, and whichever suit this card happens to be becomes trumps and will take precedence over the other three suits.

The Play The player at the dealer's left plays the first card face up and all the other players must play a card of the same suit.

The player who plays the highest card is the winner of that 'trick'. He gathers up the cards that have been played and places them in a face down packet in front of him on the table top.

A player who is unable to play a card of the same suit, may play a card of the trump suit, and so win the trick.

If players cannot play a card of the same suit and cannot play a trump card either they may play a card of any other suit. In this case they will lose the trick.

If more than one trump card is played to a trick, the highest trump card wins the trick. Any player who does not win a trick on the first round drops out of the game.

On the next round the deal passes to the next player who deals six cards only to each player and turns the next card face up in the centre. This card becomes trumps. Any player who does not win a trick drops out.

As the deal passes around the table in a clockwise direction each dealer deals one card less, until only one card is dealt to each player. The player who wins this trick is the eventual winner.

Sometimes all the players except one will drop out before the one-card situation arises, in which case the one remaining player is the winner.

Variation Instead of the winner of the last trick being the final winner, a score can be kept with pencil and paper. Then the player with the highest number of tricks to their credit is the outright winner.

Tricks with ordinary cards

Four Burglars

Effect The four Jacks are removed from the deck and displayed to the audience.

One of the Jacks is placed on the bottom of the deck. Two Jacks are now inserted into the centre of the deck and the remaining Jack is placed on top of the deck.

Hold the deck in the left hand and riffle the end of the deck with your right hand fingers. The top four cards are now turned face up to show that all four cards have gathered at the top of deck.

Method When sorting through the deck to find the four Jacks, place them at the top of the deck, with three other cards on top of them.

Remove the top seven cards from the deck and place the deck on the table. Keep the seven cards well squared up in the left hand. Take the cards in the right hand and hold them so that the face of the first Jack is facing the audience.

Now spread the four Jacks in your right hand. Keep the three other cards neatly behind the last Jack so

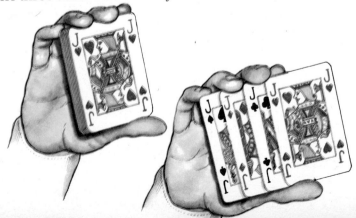

that they will not be seen. Display the four Jacks to the audience by holding them in the right hand.

Square the cards up into a neat packet and drop them on top of the deck.

Now pick off the top card of the deck, which the spectators think is a Jack, and place it on the bottom of the deck. Lift the next two cards from the top of the deck and place them in the centre of the deck.

Show that the top card of the deck is a Jack. Replace the top card on top of the deck. Pick up the deck and hold it in the left hand and give the end of the deck a riffle with the right hand fingers.

Now deal the four Jacks one at a time face up from the top of the deck on to the table.

Presentation Explain that you're going to tell a story about four burglars. The four Jacks will represent the burglars and the deck will represent the building they are going to rob.

Remove the four Jacks (plus the three other cards) and display them as described. You say, '*one of the burglars went into the basement.*' (As you say this you apparently place one of the Jacks on the bottom of the deck.)

'*Two of the burglars crawled into the first floor*'. (As you say this you apparently place two Jacks in the centre of the deck.) '*The last burglar stayed on top of the building as lookout.*'

Show the Jack on top of the deck and replace it there. '*When the lookout heard the police arrive, he signalled to the others.*' (As you say this you riffle the end of the deck.)

'*All the four burglars gathered on the roof of the building and made their getaway.*' (As you deliver the last line you deal the four Jacks off the top of the deck face up on to the table.)

An old trick, new dressing

Effect A spectator selects a card and returns it to the centre of the deck. You look through the deck quickly and find the card.

Old Method

Old Method You cut the deck at the centre and as the spectator looks at the card, you look at the bottom of the top half of the deck.

After the spectator replaces the card, you drop the top half of the deck back on top of the spectator's card. All you have to do now is to look through the deck and find the card which you had noted. The card below it is the selected card.

New Method You secretly note the name of the card on the bottom of the deck. Spread the cards and ask a spectator to remove (and remember) one card.

Ask the spectator to replace that card on top of the

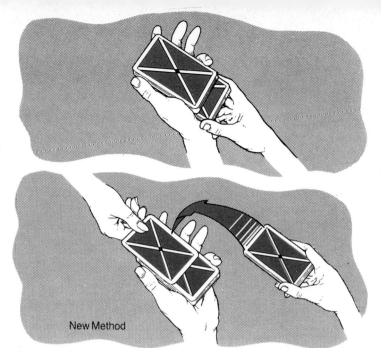

New Method

deck. Now undercut the bottom half of the deck and place it on top of the chosen card.

What you have really done is to place the bottom card (which you know) on top of the spectator's card.

Presentation After the card has been selected and returned to the centre of the deck, place the deck on the table.

Explain that there is no way in which anyone can possibly know which card has been chosen or where it is in the deck.

Pick up the deck and run through it quickly with the faces of the cards towards you. When you reach the card you have already noted, remove the card in front of it and place it on the table, face down.

Now ask the spectator to name their chosen card. Then ask them to turn the card on the table face up. It will be the same one they selected earlier!

37

Divination

THE 2 OF CLUBS THAT'S RIGHT

Effect After a spectator has cut the deck into three packets you correctly name the three cards on top.

Method You secretly note the name of the top card of the deck at the conclusion of a previous trick.

Presentation Ask someone to cut the deck into three approximately equal packets.

If the original top card (the Two of Clubs) is on top of the right hand packet, point to the left hand packet and say '*the top card is the Two of Clubs*'. Pick it up and nod as if you are correct. Place it in your left hand, face down. Do not let anyone see its face.

If the card you saw was the Ten of Spades, point to the centre packet and say '*the top card is the Ten of Spades*'.

Pick it up and nod again as if you are correct. If this card was in fact the King of Hearts, you now point to the third packet with the Two of Clubs on top and say, '*the top card is the King of Hearts*'.

Pick up the Two of Clubs, look at it and place it in your left hand with the other cards. Lay the three cards face up on the table one at a time as you name them.

38

21 Card Trick

Effect A spectator thinks of a card. You deal the cards several times and then successfully name the selected card.

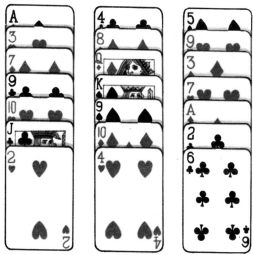

Method Deal out three rows of seven cards as shown starting at the top. Ask a spectator to think about one of the cards and to indicate which of the three rows of cards contains the chosen card.

You then gather up the cards (one row at a time), placing the row which contains the selected card between the other two.

Deal out the cards again in three rows and ask the spectator to indicate which of the three rows contains the chosen card. Gather up the three packets of cards and place the row indicated between the other two. (Do this three times in total.)

You will instantly know the name of the chosen card. It will *always* be the fourth (or central) card in the row indicated by the spectator.

Telepathic Powers

Effect This is an ideal trick to perform at a party where there are lots of people.

Ask one of your friends to leave the room for a few moments. While he or she is out spread a number of cards around on the floor, face up. Now ask a second friend to point to one of the cards.

Explain that you are going to ask the first friend to return to the room and then you'll point to several different cards. When you point to the card chosen by the second friend, the first friend will call out 'that's it!'

Emphasise that you will not speak to them nor give any secret signals—it's all done by telepathy.

Method You do in fact have a secret signal. But try as they might, your friends won't be able to discover it!

When you spread the cards (about 15 or 20) on the floor you make sure there are two or three picture cards among them.

When your friend is out of the room arrange for one card to be selected by another friend. The friend outside the room is now asked to return and you point to various cards.

The secret signal is that when you point to a picture card your friend knows that the next card will be the one selected by someone in the room.

If a picture card has been chosen as the selected card you simply point to one of the other picture cards first. Your friend will then know that the next card will be the selected one.

Presentation Explain that you and your friend have been experimenting with telepathy and want to demonstrate your amazing powers!

Variation This trick can also be performed with the cards face down. You will need a pack of cards with multicoloured backs. If there is black amongst the colours, all you have to do is point to other colours until you want to cue your confederate. You then point to the black area on the back and the next card will be the selected card.

You can also point to the top left hand corner until you cue your friend. The signal is that you point to the top right hand corner of a card and the next one is the selected card.

Overhand Shuffle Control

This shuffle can be used as a secret method of controlling a card which has been returned to the deck.

Method Ask a spectator to select a card and as they are looking at the card, start to do the Overhand shuffle (see page 8). As you are shuffling the deck, ask them to remember the card.

Now stop shuffling for a moment and extend your left hand forward (which will be holding a number of cards). Ask the spectator to replace the card on top of the cards you are holding in your left hand.

Now continue shuffling the remainder of the cards one at a time on top of this card, but as you do so remember to count the cards. After you have counted seven or eight cards, place the remaining cards from your right hand under the cards in the left hand.

You now know that the chosen card is the eighth card from the top of the deck. You can reveal the selected card in any manner you wish.

A Spelling Revelation

Effect This is a method of revealing a chosen card by means of the Overhand shuffle. You can actually find the chosen card by spelling out a spectator's name.

Method Ask a friend to select and remember a card. As he is looking at the card start to overhand shuffle the deck.

After you have shuffled a few cards from the top of deck into your left hand, extend your left hand forward and ask your friend to replace the selected card on top of those in your left hand.

After he has done this start shuffling off cards from the right hand on top of the selected card in your left hand.

If your friend's name is Robert shuffle six cards on top of the selected card. Place the remaining cards in the right hand under those held in the left hand.

Now start to spell your friend's name. Deal off one card for every letter in his name, then turn up the next card and it will be the chosen card.

R-O-B-E-R

Card Reading Extraordinary

Effect You continually name the card at the face of a deck although you never actually see the card at any time during the demonstration.

Method After a spectator has shuffled the cards take the cards and hold them behind your back for a moment. Turn the top card of the deck face up.

Bring the cards forward but make sure that the audience do not see that the top card is face up.

Hold the deck in the right hand so that the bottom card is facing the audience. In this position you can actually see the card which is reversed on top of the deck.

Explain that it would be impossible for you to know the card at the face of the deck while held in that position (but that is exactly what you are going to attempt). Place the cards behind your back again and say that you will cut the deck.

Behind your back, transfer the card you have seen on top of the deck to the face of the deck and turn the next card on top of the deck face up.

Now bring the deck forward, again being careful that the audience do not see the top card. Hold the deck up with its face to the audience and name the card which you saw previously.

At the same time look at and remember the name of the card which is now on top of the deck.

This can be repeated as often as desired.

Reds and Blacks

Effect A spectator is invited to cut a number of cards from the top of the deck and place them onto your right hand. Then by apparently weighing them, you can tell whether there is an odd or even number of cards in the packet. The effect can be repeated immediately.

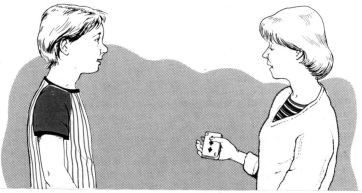

Method The cards are prearranged in order from the top of the deck to the bottom. The arrangement is simple. From the top down there is a red card then a black one, then red, then black and so on all the way through the deck.

All you have to do is note the colour of the card on the bottom of the deck, which we will assume is black.

When the spectator cuts off a packet of cards from the top of the deck and lays them on your hand, all you have to do is look at the bottom card of this packet.

If it is black, you will be holding an even number of cards. If it is red, you will be holding an odd number of cards.

Tricks with special cards
2 from 5 Leaves??

Effect Five cards are shown to the audience and dropped into a hat or box on the table. You reach into the hat and openly remove two cards one at a time and place them aside. Now ask the spectators how many cards are left in the hat. They will naturally answer, 'three'.

Now lift the hat from the table and turn it towards the audience to show that it is empty. The cards have disappeared completely.

Reach into your pocket and produce the three missing cards.

Method You cut the left hand sections from the King, Queen and Jack of Hearts and paste them on to the Ace of Hearts.

Take another Ace of Hearts and paste this on to the back of the first Ace of Hearts. You will also need a Ten of Hearts plus another Jack, Queen and King of Hearts.

Preparation Place the Ace of Hearts, with its normal face down, into the hat. On top of the Ace, place the Ten of Hearts, face up. The duplicate Jack, Queen and King, are placed in the jacket pocket.

Presentation Reach into the hat and take out what is apparently a small packet of cards. Spread the cards out to show that they are the Ace, Jack, Queen, King, and Ten of Hearts. Hold them in your left hand.

Pick up the hat with your right hand and show the inside of the hat, then replace it on the table. Drop the cards into the hat with the left hand. Reach into the hat and remove the Ten of Hearts with your right hand and place it aside.

Repeat the action and remove the special card from the hat showing the Ace of Hearts side to the audience and place this card aside.

Ask the audience how many cards are left in the hat and they will answer, 'three'. Lift the hat to show that it is empty. Now produce the missing three cards from your jacket pocket.

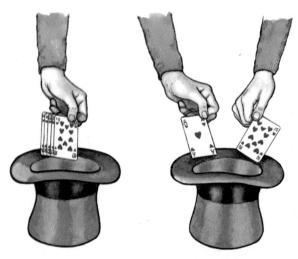

The Dissolving Card

Effect A freely selected card is inserted into a glass of water and disappears completely.

Method You will need a piece of clear plastic or celluloid exactly the same size, shape and thickness as a playing card, a glass of water, a deck of cards and a pocket handkerchief.

The glass should be of the clear variety and not coloured but should if possible have some kind of pattern or design on its surface. (A patterned glass will help to hide the card.) If the transparent card is inserted into the glass of water it will apparently vanish from sight.

Preparation The transparent card should be on the table with the handkerchief covering it. The glass of water is placed in the centre of the table.

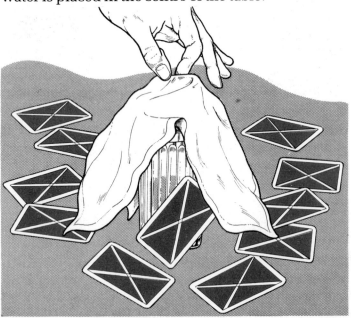

Presentation Ask someone to select a card from anywhere in the deck. Now scatter the deck face down on the table top all around the glass. As you do so, point out that they had a free choice of card.

Take the card from the spectator and lift the edge of the handkerchief with your left hand while placing the card under it with your right hand.

Now take hold of the card and the transparent card through the handkerchief and hold them as one card with your left hand and raise the handkerchief clear of the table top.

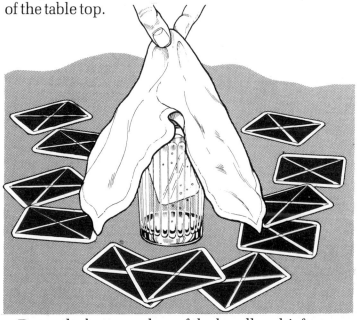

Drape the bottom edges of the handkerchief over the glass. As this is done, your left hand releases its grip on the card and drops it on to the table top where it will lie face down on top of all the other cards which are scattered about.

Push the transparent card down into the glass with your left hand. Remove the handkerchief after a moment to show that the card has vanished.

Juggling Trick

Effect One playing card is balanced on the top of another.

Method A special card called a 'flap card' is used to achieve this effect. The illustration will make it easier to understand.

To make this 'flap card' you will need three cards. Drop two of the cards into a bowl of water and leave them there to soak for a while. You will now find it's easy to peel the backs from the cards.

When you have done this, place them between the pages of an old book and leave them to dry. When they are dry, fold both cards in half lengthways. Paste the two cards together as shown and then paste both of them to the back of the third card.

You have now made a flap which can be folded flat in either direction.

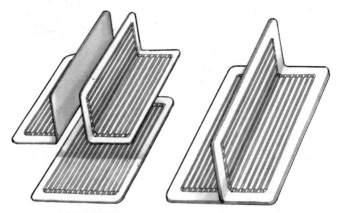

The backs of two cards are peeled off, folded and stuck onto a third card.

Preparation Place the 'flap card' on top of the deck.

Presentation Remove the 'flap card' from the top of the deck and hold it in the left hand. As you do this pull the flap out with your left forefinger so that it is at right angles to the front of the card.

Remove another card from the deck and lay it on top of the 'flap card'. The 'flap card' will stand up and the ordinary card will look as if it is being balanced on the top edge of a single card. The ordinary card can now be moved around and appears to balance at odd angles.

To bring the trick to an end just blow the card off the 'flap card' so that it flutters to the floor. As this happens, close the flap and place the 'flap card' in your pocket.

One-way Deck

This trick is included in this section because you may
have to look around to find this kind of deck.

Effect A spectator selects a card from the deck and
replaces it anywhere in the deck. The spectator then
shuffles the deck. You now run through the deck very
quickly and find the spectator's card.

Method You will require a deck of cards which has a
pictorial back design which can only be viewed one
way. If one of the cards is reversed in the deck, it can
be found very easily by running through the deck and
looking at the back design.

Preparation Arrange the deck so that all the picture
designs on the back are facing the same way.

Presentation Invite someone to select a card, and
while they are looking at the card, turn the deck
around in your hands, end for end. Spread the deck
and ask him to replace the card anywhere he likes in
the deck. Then ask him to shuffle the cards.

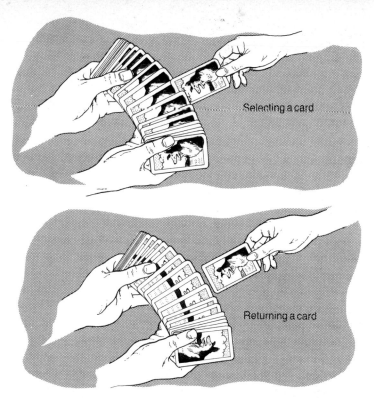

Selecting a card

Returning a card

Take the cards from him and turn your back for a moment. When you face him again you should be holding the deck in your left hand with one card in the right hand. This card is the selected card.

Important If you perform several other card tricks first, make a note of how the spectator shuffles the cards. If he uses the normal overhand shuffle, you can safely allow him to shuffle the deck.

If he uses any other kind of shuffle there is a possibility that he may mix up the back designs. If this is the case, do not allow him to shuffle the cards. Mix them up yourself after he has replaced his card in the deck and use the overhand shuffle. This will ensure that the cards will remain one way.

Fortune Telling (1)

This is a very simple system for telling fortunes as pure entertainment.

As you know there are four suits in a deck of cards. There are Hearts, Clubs, Spades and Diamonds. In card fortune telling each card has a special meaning according to its value and suit.

Here are a few ideas for remembering the meaning of each card.

Love

Play

Work

Money

Unhappy

Happy

3 Lucky

4 Unlucky

5 Countryside

6 City centre

7 Travel

8 Gate

9 Rope

10 Farmyard

J Stranger

Q Lady

K Tall Man

Surprise (Joker)

Fortune Telling (2)

From the ideas on pages 54 and 55 you will see that it's quite simple to make up a short story from just one card.

For instance, if a Three of Diamonds shows up you say the Three means 'lucky' and Diamonds means 'money'.

You could tell the person that they are going to win some money or someone will give them money or they may even find some money.

If a King of Clubs shows up you can tell them that '*a tall man is going to become involved with them in their leisure time*'. And so on...

If you want to make up a longer story you could do the following. Remove the Joker from the deck. Place it to one side and shuffle the cards thoroughly.

Ask a friend for the year of her birth. If it's 1969, you deal out one card for the ONE. Next to this you deal out nine cards on top of each other for the NINE. Then you deal out six cards for the SIX and finally another nine cards for the final NINE.

Turn the top card of each packet face up and create a short story from them.

If the cards are Six of Clubs, Ace of Hearts, Ten of Diamonds and Two of Spades, the chart will give you a clue as to what to say. Here are some ideas.

You are going to the City Centre for pleasure.

You are going to be unhappy in love.

A visit to a farm will involve you in money.

You are going to be happy at work.

You could say something like this.

'*Things are going to improve for you at work (or*

school) and as a result you will be rewarded by an evening out in town. Do not get involved romantically at present as things may not work out too well for you. You will become financially involved in a farm project.'

If there is a Zero in the year of birth, place the Joker in that Zero position. This means they are in for a big surprise!

The stories can be as varied as you wish. Just use your imagination!

Passé Passé Cards

Effect The Ace of Diamonds is placed into a hat on the left of a table. The Ace of Spades is placed into a hat on the right of a table. On command, the two cards change places. The Ace of Diamonds is removed from the hat on the right and the Ace of Spades is removed from the hat on the left. Both hats are now empty.

Method Four cards are used in this effect. Take two Aces of Spades and two Aces of Diamonds. Paste the Diamonds onto the backs of the Spades. You now have two cards only, each with the Ace of Spades on one side and the Ace of Diamonds on the other.

Preparation Put two hats on the table. One Ace of Diamonds and one Ace of Spades should be on the table face up.

Presentation Show the audience the empty hats. Pick up the Ace of Diamonds in the left hand and the Ace of Spades in the right hand and display them to the audience. Make sure that they do not see the other sides of the cards.

Put the cards into the hats and after you have 'commanded' them to change places reach into the hats. Remove the cards but as you do so turn the cards over so that the other faces are showing. Place the cards on the table. Show the empty hats to the audience.

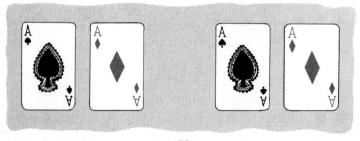

The Soldier's Bible

Here is a story about a soldier who was arrested in church for playing cards. In his defence he is supposed to have said these words:

'To me this deck of cards is my Holy Bible. When I look through the cards and see an Ace, it reminds me that there is but one God in Heaven and Earth.

When I see a Two it tells me that the Bible is divided into two parts, the Old and the New Testaments.

The Three, that there are three persons in the Holy Trinity – the Father, the Son and the Holy Ghost. The Four reminds me of Matthew, Mark, Luke and John, the four great evangelists who wrote the Gospels.

The Five denotes the Five Wise Virgins who trimmed their lamps against the coming of the Messiah.

The Six, that the Lord made Heaven and Earth in six days and the Seven, that he rested on the seventh day.

The Eight conveys to me that Noah, his wife, their three sons and their wives were all saved from the Great Flood.

The Nine tells me not to be as ungrateful as the nine lepers who were cleansed by Our Lord.

The Ten is the Ten Commandments which were brought down from the mountain by Moses.

The sight of the Knave (Jack) warns me to shun temptation from the Devil.

The Queen reminds me of the Queen of Sheba who doubted the wisdom of Solomon. The King counsels me to bow down and worship the one true King of all Heaven and Earth.

I may add sir, if I count the spots in any deck of cards they will add up to 365 and there are 365 days in the year.

The Joker represents the one extra day in a leap year. There are 52 cards in the deck and 52 weeks in a year.

There are 13 cards to a suit and 13 lunar months in a year. The four suits represent the four seasons – Spring, Summer, Autumn and Winter. The red and black colours of the suits denote night and day.

So you see this deck of cards is not only my Bible but my Almanac.'

Reference section

Glossary

Ace high: The ace has the highest value of the thirteen cards.

Bullet: An ace.

Burn: To bury a card in the centre of the deck.

Cut: To divide the deck into two portions by lifting off the upper half.

Complete the cut: To place the lower half of the deck on top of the upper half after the deck has been cut.

Card sharp or card shark: A person who cheats at cards.

Doublefaced: A card which has a value printed on both sides of the card.

Doublebacked: A card which has a back design printed on both sides of the card.

Deck: Refers to the whole fifty-two cards.

Deuce: A card with a value of two.

Deal: To distribute the cards between the players.

Dealer: The person who distributes the cards.

Dead card: A card which is not used in a game.

Draw: To pick a card from the deck.

Force: To make a spectator take the card of your choice.

Fake (Feke) cards: Cards which have been specially prepared by printing, cutting etc.

Flush: A number of cards of the same suit.

Hand: The cards a player holds during a game.

Indices: The number and suit of a card which are printed in the corners of the card.

Kitty: The total of money, sweets or matchsticks contributed by the players as a prize for winning.

Mental trick: A magic trick where the performer apparently has telepathic powers.

One-way deck: A deck of cards with a distinctive back design which can only be viewed when the back design is the right way up.

Pack: Another name for a 'deck of cards'.

Packet: Any number of cards less than fifty-two.

Peek: To secretly look at the face of a card.

Palm: To secretly hold a card in the palm of your hand.

Pasteboards: Another name for playing cards.

Picture card: Any Jack, Queen or King.

Books

Pass: Not to participate at that point in the game.

Pair: Two cards of the same value.

Royal flush: The Ten, Jack, Queen, King and Ace of one suit.

Run: A number of cards with their values in sequence.

Spot card: Any card which is not a picture card.

Self-working: Any effect (trick) which does not require sleight of hand.

Shuffle: To mix the cards.

Sleight: A secret handling of a card or cards which is unseen by the audience.

Stake: The amount a player deposits in the kitty.

Trick: An apparently magical happening.

Trey: A card with a value of three.

Three of a kind: Three cards of the same value.

Undercut: To remove the lower half of the deck and place it on top of the upper half while the cards are held in the hand.

The Complete Card Player
by A.A. Ostrow
(The Bodley Head).

Card Games by D. Parlett
(Penguin)

Complete Illustrated Book of Card Tricks by
W. Gibson (Kaye & Ward).

Card Manipulations
by J. Hugard (Davenport).

Card Tricks for Beginners
by H. Baron (Kaye & Ward).

Royal Road to Card Magic
by J. Hugard & F. Braue
(Faber).

Card Conjuring
by W. Johnson (Foyles).

Encyclopedia of Card Tricks by J. Hugard
(Faber).

Card Tricks Without Skill
by Paul Clive (Faber).

Tricks with Cards
by P. Page (Wolfe).

Hofzinser's Card Conjuring by O. Fischer
(Johnson).

Shops and suppliers

L. Davenport & Co.,
51 Great Russell Street,
London, WC2.

Alan Alan's Magic Spot,
88 Southampton Row,
London, WC2.

Repro Magic,
46 Queenstown Road,
London, SW11.

Supreme Magic Co.,
64 High Street,
Bideford,
Devon.

Taurus Magic Supplies,
146 Walmersley Road,
Bury,
Lancashire.

Terry Burgess,
6 Fulham Field,
Hatch End,
Pinner,
Middlesex.

R.A.R. Magic,
82 Pennard Drive,
Pennard,
Swansea.

International Magic,
89 Clerkenwell Road,
London, EC1.

Magic Books by Post,
29 Hill Avenue,
Bedminster,
Bristol.

Kovari Magic,
465 Watford Way,
London, NW4.

Murray's Magic Mart,
27 Cookson Street,
Blackpool.

Tam Shepherd,
33 Queen Street,
Glasgow, C1.

Paul Scott Magic,
177 Churchill Parade,
Birchfield Road,
Perry Barr,
Birmingham.

Societies

The Magic Circle,
84 Cenies Mews,
London, WC1.

International Brotherhood of Magicians,
Secretary, 'The Wand',
Dudsbury Crescent,
Wimborne,
Dorset.

British Magical Society,
Secretary, B. Gordon,
125 Whitecrest,
Great Barr,
Birmingham.

Index

The **numbers** in **bold** denote the ideal number of players for a game.

G = game, T = trick.